How to Use
Positive Brain Training
On The
Journey to "True Success"
P-1

Visit our Web site at www.MichaelsonWilliams.com

Printed in the United States of America

ISBN-13: 978-0615926162

ISBN-10: 0615926169

How to Use

Positive Brain Training

On The

Journey to "True Success"

By: Michaelson Williams

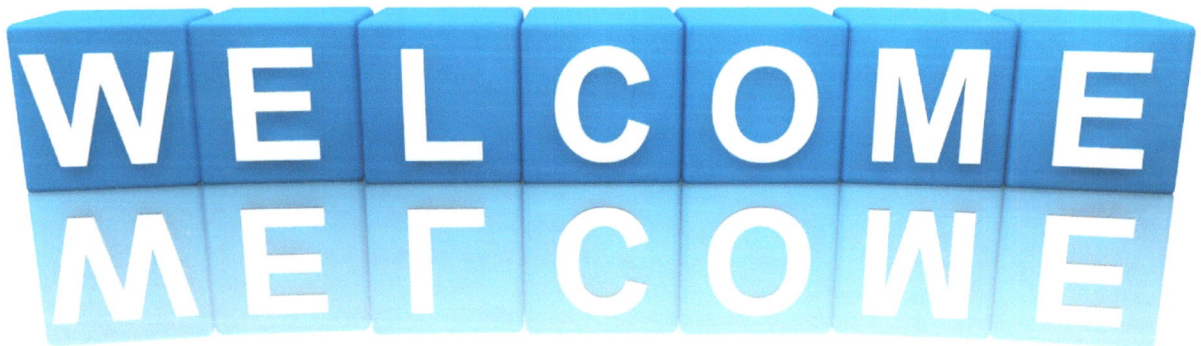

Introduction

This short guide will outline small tips and tricks which will increase one's level of the achievement on the journey to "True Success". Every one of these tips is based on the principles of Trainwashing and the Secrets of Positive Brain Washing. While reading this, I want you to keep in mind the word brainwashing does not have to invoke a sense of fear or negativity in your mind.

Look at the word brainwashing from a different perspective. The word or the action of brainwashing can also be thought of as a positive helpful success driven action. When you think of the word brainwashing from now on put the word positive in front of it. Now you have the words positive brainwashing.

Now in addition to how we think of the words positive brainwashing we must think about how it applies to our own control. Therefore, when we think about positive brainwashing think about it in a manner in which you have complete control over this process.

When having complete control over the positive brainwashing process there is little to no fear. In other words the negative perception of the word brainwashing or negative mind control is eliminated. We want to have control over our own mind and I've found the best way to do this is to positively brainwash yourself. Moreover it is possible to change a great deal of negative thought into positive thinking through my system of positive brainwashing.

Positive brainwashing is nothing more than a tool to bring a sub-positive mind into an extremely positive place. "Trainwashing" is a series of applicable principles which allows full control over the journey to "True Success" through positive conditioning. When the mind is void of negativity then positive actions can be taken to improve one's life.

We are all looking for a better life and a better way for our family. It is very difficult to understand how to achieve "better" when using a mind that has been conditioned to fail. Now there's nothing wrong with failure because it teaches us lessons we then use to change our direction. Therefore, conceptually we need a certain amount of failure in our life to help us grow into more positive foundation people. However, there is an issue with our society today; regarding how much we fail and accept failure within ourselves.

When we are not in control of our own positive thinking then the majority of time our subconscious is focused on feeding us constant negativity. The unconscious mind works on a system running on autopilot. Therefore, there is little attentiveness to the negativity conditioning in the background. When the awareness of negativity is apparent, it is usually a fleeting thought which we try to talk ourselves out of in the moment.

The problem with the action previously mentioned is we are talking ourselves out of the negative conditioning with our conscious mind. The conscious mind is not powerful enough in its normal, untrained state to correct the negative path. If, and when, the conscious mind is able to release us from negative thoughts, it is short lived.

In other words, the conscious mind doesn't have the strength in its current state to supersede the lifetime of negative conditioning that has gone on in our life. If we could use the conscious mind to settle all of our past issues and negativity, then it would take just a split-second. The only thing we would have to say to ourselves is "I do not want to be negative any more". Then with this action from our conscious mind the deed would be complete and only positive thoughts would occur. Unfortunately our minds return to the perception of normality which is usually negative for most.

After saying positive affirmations just-like-magic our lives will be changed. But as we all know this never happens because we've all tried this action and found it didn't work. If our perception told us affirmations did work, we could understand it was just an instant and then we returned back to our "normal" state. This normal state of being is run by our subconscious mind. Because our subconscious mind runs on autopilot and has been systematically negatively conditioned, we live in a world truly not our own. Yes, we live in a fantasy world.

There is absolutely nothing wrong with living in a fantasy world as long as you have the ability to create a world bringing you everything you want in life. There is also nothing wrong with living in a fantasy world if you are the person who created the fantasy and had complete control over this fantasy. We have all had dreams of being someone greater than who we are now. This is intrinsic behavior in humans. Of course the fantasy then becomes reality hence laser focus should be on positive thinking.

However, if someone else is the puppet master and controlling your perception of life then there can be no positive fantasy. Everything believed would be to someone else's gain corporations, mega-wealthy, government, etc. My **Expanding Trainwashing coursework** acts as a conduit in the task of breaking negative feelings, emotions, training, and actions in order to retrain the same but in a positive manner. Expanding Trainwashing systematically puts you back in the driver seat of your own life and successes.

Depending on how ingrained the negative conditioning is for the individual, the tips within the pages of this guide may be either extremely helpful, not as much. Because we are different people our levels of negativity are always different. The way we handle different negativities in our lives is varies due to our dissimilar upbringing and past journey.

Nevertheless, try to put these tips into practice in your daily life working diligently to use your conscious mind to retrain the negative subconscious. The full coursework and My 100% Lifetime Guarantee in the achievement of "True Success" can be found at www.MichaelsonWilliams.com. In short this guarantee states if you take my Platinum VIP membership courses you will build a better life and achieve Greater Successes! If not, it's Free.

Now, before we get started, I want you to start realizing a few things. *Now is the time to improve your life!* This improvement should have a serious sense of urgency. There is no gain in waiting. You cannot move forward if you're always waiting around for a savior or the end of the world. Whatever it is keeping you from moving forward on your journey, release it and get moving. Stop waiting and hoping for something to give you direction and make your own path. Be the trailblazer in your own success on this journey!

I can guarantee you this one thing: if you do not take actions in life, nothing will happen. On the other hand, if you start taking action now; I absolutely *guarantee* positive things will start happening. I know this for a fact because that is the way it works. Unless there is an energy pushing from some direction an object in a seemingly empty space cannot move on its own. Actions must be taken in life and belief in your own due diligence must be realized in order to trust the path you've taking.

When you start to falter, and you will because most of us second-guess our decisions many times-keep moving in a positive direction. Do not allow yourself to take backward steps because of fear. Trust you are on the right path and keep taking "baby steps" forward until the low times have passed.

Give yourself the "Green Light" in your mind to believe success is acceptable. If you are going to have faith, have faith in yourself and in your ability to achieve greater than what you have at this point in your life. Stand on your own 2 feet and stop waiting for others to do the job you should be doing yourself. Realize your own greatness and greatness will come to you, I guarantee it!

Now Let's Get Started

Give Yourself
The Green Light
Become a Total Success

<u>Journey Tip Number One</u>

Focus daily on the belief that within you is a level of greatness allowing the achievement of everything you want in life. Your lifelong negative conditioning has tricked you into believing you are less than what you really are in life. This clearly is a lie. Obviously, you possess greatness! Your mind is stuck in the place of limbo most of the time and this is due to its conditioning.

The paths we have chosen which cause us to believe we're moving forward are usually causing us to chase our own tails. Therefore, when we do get a chance to assess our life the perception is that we do not have enough. These beliefs must be changed to thoughts such as "I am great already and able to achieve anything."

How do we accomplish this task?

Each and every day when we wake up in the morning say out loud the words "I Am Great!" Say "I Feel Fantastic!" Repeat the words "I am wealthy in mind, body, spirit, and "I Can Achieve Anything I Want in Life!". Rehearse this each and every day with your conscious mind until it becomes unconscious actions.

<u>Journey Tip Number Two</u>

What's on your mind and what do you think about for the majority of your day? Are you completely consumed by your troubles or what you consider "drama" in your life? Do you find you have a very difficult time focusing on positive things in your life? How many times do you catch yourself in an angered state, not knowing the source of the emotion?

How often do you find enjoyment in life to be short lived or fleeting? If these questions bring up negative emotions, then your sustained thoughts are controlled by how you feel **right now**. The thoughts you keep on your mind for the longest time and what you think about dictates your life. Therefore, if the major focus is on negativity, you are going to live in a negatively created world for yourself.

How do we solve this problem?

We must change our perception of who we are today. Once this perception has changed then we can create the person who we want to be tomorrow. There is a voice which tells us something is wrong with our life in the state of mind we're in right now. Sometimes this voice is little and can barely be heard; and other times it's shouting in great alarm. We must listen intently so actions can be taken in order to create a positive new you.

The "new you" is a successful more in control person. This person is inside of everyone and has always been there. However most of us have lost contact with this side of us. Start changing what you think about by reverse engineering your thoughts of the day. This will initiate the new positive changes as you recognize the negative self-speak.

<u>Journey Tip Number Three</u>

One issue which can hold us back from being successful is the fact there's unwillingness within some of us to help others. We were not born with this unwillingness to help others. Think back to when you were a child and how generous you were. Even though there were times when selfishness was displayed, it was most likely short-lived. Then you eventually shared whatever it was you had with someone else.

When we were children, it was fun for us to share with others because it brought us joy in our little lives. The sharing behavior came once we found basic survival instinct were less of a necessity. We must return to this state of mind by helping others in our life today. When helping others even in the slightest manner a chemical reaction occurs in which help us to experience joy. On the other hand not helping or harming someone in need causes negative reaction from the body whether it is internal or external.

How do we help others so we can help ourselves?

It's pretty simple, find something you're really good at and then teach it to someone else. If you think you are not good at anything, learn something. That's basically all it takes and you do not even have to be an expert. What you will find is if you are not an expert but start teaching someone expertise will come quickly.

The reason you become an expert quickly is because spending more time doing a particular task means the task becomes easier. The brain learns very quickly when you are helping someone else. I do hours of free mentoring and this brings me up in happiness and gratefulness while on my journey. Taking these types of actions will do the same for you.

Expanding Trainwashing Leads to Positive

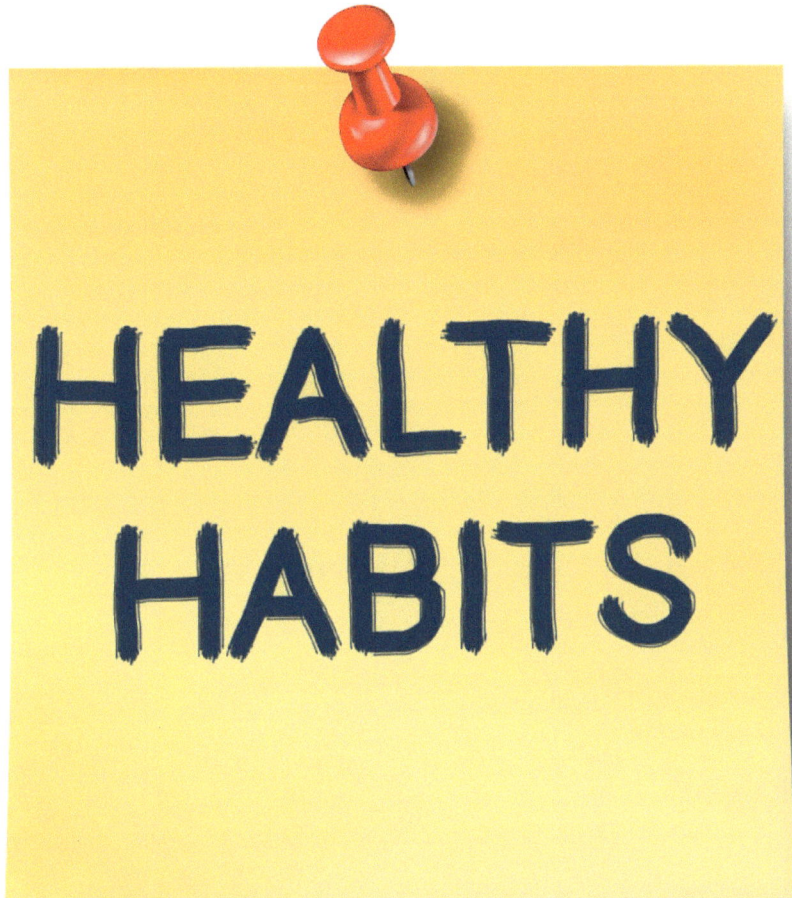

Journey Tip Number Four

Do not let the Ego interrupt your positive journey to true success. The ego is the interference which will create havoc in your life. This emotional havoc will keep you stuck exactly where you're at right now. When having selfish, bad thoughts or feel as if someone has done some type of wrong to you, this is your ego. Remember this is part of the negative perception we have about life.

Start trying to understand the ego so you can look at the world without the "knife in your back" emotions. If you continue to engage life with "ego" it will always seem as if someone is out to get you. If the mind is focused on thinking someone is out to take from you, you cannot move forward positively. You will be stuck focused on negativity, hatred, and how NOT to be able to accomplish true success.

How to eliminate ego while on the journey?

Eliminating ego is fairly simple once you understand and recognize when ego is causing havoc in your life. Use what I call the "3E's" Ego to Enthusiasm through Expansion. The way it works is: as you become expanded you start to see ego as it really appears. Once ego is understood, only then will enthusiasm work as a replacement. However, early on you won't be able to stop Ego because it's like a train wreck. Once a train wreck is in motion almost nothing can change its course. You end up waiting for the train wreck to be over and then seeing what damage was caused in the aftermath.

After some time, research, and mental exercise you will find you are able to understand the ego better. Once you understand your own ego you will be able to basically "head off at the pass". The way you will learn to do this is to replace ego with enthusiasm.

Using the **"3E's"** the effects of the ego will not be as imposed. The ego cannot live in a body that is full of enthusiasm, it doesn't work. Therefore every time you feel the effect of ego creeping in and you recognize it, replace the ego with enthusiasm. Always continue to seek expansion at time of ego because an enemy understood is easily defeated. You will be ahead of the game and one step closer to "True Success"!

Journey Tip Number Five

Unfortunately or fortunately depending on how you look at it we have to understand and admit we have been brainwashed and negatively conditioned most of life. Moreover there should be some understanding we could be one of the negatively brainwashed and negatively conditioned right now.

Once we are able to admit this fact then we will have the power to start the positive self brain training process. Now I should've put this at an earlier position of the guide, maybe even at the number one position. However I didn't think it would fare well there as most of us reject the truth at first glance. At this point you either admit or you quit right now because this journey is not for you.

After admitting negative conditioning is possible and is happening then what?

Once we have admitted to this brainwashing and negative conditioning it is time to make positive changes. Now it is time to counteract the many years of negative conditioning that's been part of your life since childhood. Now you are; by continue reading this information taking positive steps to truly change your life for the better and I applaud you.

Continue to seek and research in order to open your mind to allow your own greatness to be released. It is a wonderful experience to have understanding you cannot fail in life. I want everyone to feel as if (failure is just not an option) because within an unchained mind, is the absolute truth.

Journey Tip Number Six

Life is a journey and it is one you should **Never Give Up** on. Because life is a journey and we are conditioned to believe everything should come instantaneously; we find giving up to be easy. I find people want to give up on everything in life. People want everything to be given to them overnight without a bit of work. And then when this perceived want comes and isn't perfect it was someone else's fault.

If there is a business related deal and money isn't made immediately then "it was a scam". Well there are no scams, only un-researched information. No one can pull the wool over the eyes of an informed person. Use due diligence in order to plan your path to true success. Once the past has been set and the initial work has been put in move forward without hesitation.

What does it mean to "Never Give Up"?

Never giving up means to take whatever steps needed to accomplish a goal. The goal need not be large. If you are studying **Expanding Trainwashing Courses** you know every goal should be small. How large or small the goal matters to your conscious mind. If your conscious mind sees the goal as something unattainable this increases the chances of quitting.

However making steps which are so small the conscious mind is unable to focus on will allow the actions of the subconscious to accomplish the goal for you. Therefore never give up because the energy you put in to the initial work will reveal itself through the actions of the unconscious mind.

Journey Tip Number Seven

Make sure you are happy for as much of the day and every day from here on out. From this point on make sure you do things which bring you happiness and happiness to the ones closest to you. Spend time with people who make you happy! Attend events that make you happy! Eliminate things which make you dull or unhappy.

So how do we make ourselves happy all the time?

Even as expansion begins through the **Expanding Trainwashing Coursework** it is still going to be difficult to be happy all the time. There is a part of man's intrinsic way which makes us believe having pain in our lives is a normal part of being human. As long as we believe we are nothing more than human then happiness can only be a fraction of our experience.

The key is to make sure the happiness parts of your life is the prevalent part of life. Simply put; do whatever it takes to keep you in a happy mindset because you will generate bigger and better energy. When your energy is happy you will do happy things and happy people will come your way.

Journey Tip Number Eight

Never allow fear to take over your journey. You create your own fear and without you fear cannot exist. The problem with creating fear or fear not existing is; we are part of the creation process through your conscious thoughts. Through our conscious thoughts we create fear which reveals itself through inaction on the journey to "True Success".

Keep in mind this is not the same fear mechanisms which show through the primitive side of mankind. I am talking about the irrelevant and irrational fears which have been conditioned in to your mind. Fear will stop you dead in your tracks and grow taller than the largest tree you've ever seen, if you let it.

Fear can cause you to think negative things are in your life that is not really there. Fear can cause rationalizations that will lock the mind into believing something which is completely irrational. Fear will completely control the way you live your life and if you let it; halt any forward movement on the journey to true success.

How do we eliminate fear?

The way you eliminate fear is to put things that scare you in front of you as often as possible. Anything you fear, do it, make it happen, put it in front of you and it will become less. Our fears are based on our perception of live. This why one person may fear snakes and another person places the snake over his or her shoulders.

If the snake fearing person manages to put the snake on their shoulders the perception is changed and fear become less. How much less is dependent on the person and their acceptance of the new perception of the snake. Once you have eliminated one fear find one perceived to be larger. Expanding Trainwashing eliminates one fear after the other until irrational positive movement fears on the journey to true success are gone.

<u>Journey Tip Number Nine</u>

Being positive on the journey to success is as important as any other principle of Trainwashing. If you cannot be positive for yourself and for others your journey is going to be very difficult. Negativity comes through negative self-talk or the negative conversation we have with ourselves. If we are always speaking negatively in our own head there can be nothing more than a negative person on the outside.

If your conversation with yourself is filled with negativity you will not possess the power in order to be positive on the outside. No matter what it takes change your internal conversation from negative to positive, from ego to Enthusiastic using the "3E's". Fill the spaces of your life with positive things, positive reading, and positive self-programming. Plain and simply you will start transitioning into a positive person.

How do we become more positive?

The best ways to ensure you are a positive person is to slowly evaluate and then eliminate negative training or conditioning from your life. One way to eliminate negative conditioning and brainwashing is to eliminate the number of hours of television watched each day. It is statistically known the more television you watch the lower your income level.

I'll let you in on a little secret here; the mega-wealthy do not watch a great deal of television. When the ultra-rich do decide to watch television they choose very wisely of its programming. Now ask yourself why would this be? The answer to this question is; television facilitates negative conditioning through informing you of every negative incident in the world. This is not to mention the primetime unrealistic programming of "Reality TV", etc, etc.

In Plain Sight

In my book Trainwashing: The Secrets of Positive Brain Washing I reveal a book the mega-wealthy used to ensure wealth stays in their family for multiple generations. Yes, if you thought you were out of the loop when it comes to creating financial success, you were right.

Although this book is available to the general public it is not shared openly but only to a few. One would think if this book is so important to the Ultra-Wealthy it would be needed by everyone. Moreover this book made part of every school in America teaching curriculum. If you are not specifically looking for this particular book you are likely not to know of its existence.

The book in question is a roadmap to becoming and keeping great wealth for multiple generations. It took me years of research to put my **Expanding Trainwashing Coursework** together so I could guarantee True Success to anyone. It was through this research process I found this ultra-wealthy success book. If I had not gone down this path and been on this journey I would have never found and read this book. Now I'm sharing this books information and these principles with you as part of my philosophy of Trainwashing.

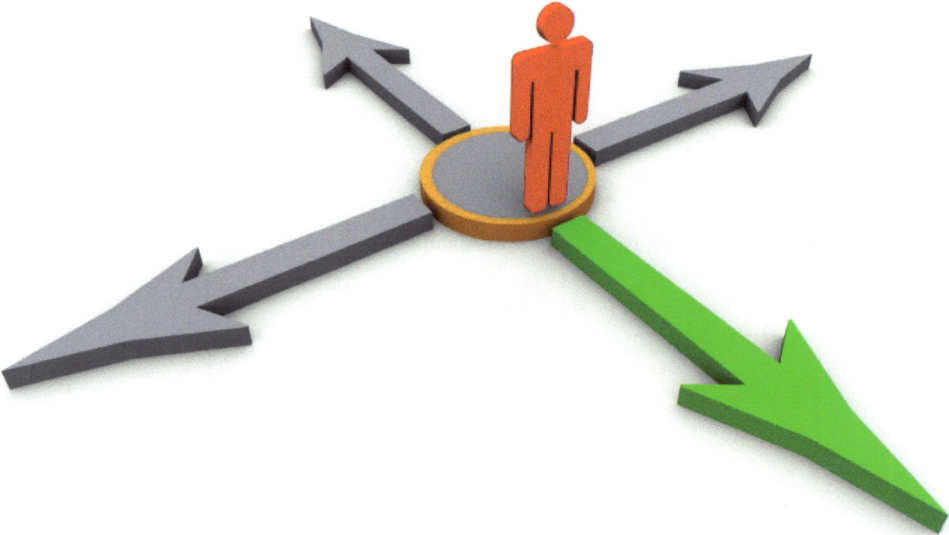

My Research:

Here is some interesting research on the effects of television on children. This article is the most credible one I could find without bias or seeking my own truth. I speak more about the effects of finding truths which only coincide with one's own emotion and perception in the Expanding Trainwashing lectures. This research information is from the website http://www.ithaca.edu/cretv/research/tv_lives.html

Article Title: "*Television in the Lives of Children*"

Author: Cyndy Scheibe

"The following suggestions are based on our experiences with children and our research on media literacy, and also include information from several published sources concerning the effects of television on children. A list of these and other excellent readings is given at the end of this handout, and if you are interested in reading more about this topic, we highly recommend them.

In general, the effects of television on viewers can be divided into two different types: 1) direct effects due to the content of what is seen (in the programs or commercials); and 2) indirect effects due to the activity of watching TV, regardless of what is being watched. This second type of effect is very important, because it usually means that the more time children spend watching TV, the less time they are spending doing other important activities (like reading, talking with others, getting exercise, playing games, being outdoors, etc.). A lot of the negative effects of TV, like lower reading scores, obesity, and poor physical fitness, seem to be due to these indirect effects. Because of that, it's probably important to set some limits on the amount of time your child spends watching TV, regardless of what shows you allow them to watch. Remember, four hours of Sesame Street is still four hours of television.

We've found that most parents are concerned about violence on TV and its effects on their children. Television does include a lot of violence, not only on adult crime dramas, but also on cartoons, on slapstick comedies, and on the nightly news. The psychological research that has been done in this area over the last 20 years has shown three general effects of watching TV violence: 1) children may become less sensitive to the pain and suffering of others, both on television and in real life; 2) children may be more fearful of the world around them; and 3) children may be more likely to behave in aggressive or harmful ways toward others. The impact of TV violence on aggression seems to be partly due to imitation of the aggressive actions that children see (particularly if they are done by the "good guys") and partly due to the messages that aggression works to get what you want and it's OK to use aggression if you are justified in doing so (a message we get a lot in adult crime shows). Because of these findings, you may want to set"—

To read more check out the website link.

http://www.ithaca.edu/cretv/research/tv_lives.html

Journey Tip Number Ten

By creating a **Vision-board** you are setting up visual roadmap to what you will achieve in life. If you do not know what a vision-board is; it is a collage of pictures in which is hung up as a reminder of successes you wish to achieve. The vision-board works as visual stimulation to the subconscious mind.

Vision-boards do not have to be elaborate, but they do have to be true to whom you are in the future, not who you are currently. If you create a vision-board based on current self perceptions, you will have a difficult time achieving what you want to achieve. Therefore, the first exercise in creating a vision-board is creating thoughts of how you see yourself in the very near future. Envision yourself as educated, loving, strong, wealthy, successful, financially free, grateful, abundant, and full of joy.

Created correctly and the vision-board along with the other expansion work acts as a time machine of sorts. In time, the right time you will wake wondering how it was you hadn't achieved this wealth sooner. However, continue to hold fast to what you think you know and the vision-board is nothing more than the reflecting of the broken you.

How do I create a Vision-board?

Start creating your vision-board by creating a dream life for yourself. In this dream life think of everything you will have and then imagine how you will feel when you have it. Once you have done this, select pictures from magazines, books, the Internet, etc. as representation of this life. Make sure these pictures representations are of your new life not the life you have right now. Understanding through the proper education and retraining of mind these things will come to you automatically.

The absolutely amazing thing about Expanding Trainwashing is that the emotional stimulation of the law of attraction is automatic. Therefore by using this course the actions needed to achieve "True Success" happens through a new positively condition autopilot subconscious. Once the subconscious is Trainwashed properly failure and lack of success is not an option.

I am extremely excited you have completed the reading of this information! I am even more elated that you have chosen this path on your journey of true enlightenment and expansion which will lead you to True Success!

Success still isn't Easy but NOW it's Guaranteed!

The Bottom Line

If your mind is not in the right place the road to success is going to be difficult, and the road to "True Success" is going to be nearly impossible.

Guarantee Your "True Success" Today!

So what's the Solution?

My Positive Brain Training Courses For

"True Success"

is the Answer.

Expanding Trainwashing

To continue your journey with Me visit: http://MichaelsonWilliams.com and sign up as a VIP Member. This will give you different levels of access to my Positive Brain Training-Expanding Trainwashing courses. Also you will find my 100% Positive Brain Training Lifetime Guarantee for Platinum VIP Members.

I'll See You Inside!

References:

Williams, M. (2013).Trainwashing: The Secrets of Positive Brain Washing ch.15 p.131-134., Digital Retrieval From http://www.michaelsonwilliams.com

Scheibe, C. (2013). Center for Research on the Effects of Television. Retrieved From http://www.ithaca.edu/cretv/research/tv_lives.html

www.ingramcontent.com/pod-product-compliance
Lightning Source LLC
Chambersburg PA
CBHW041236040426

42445CB00004B/52